The Things You Can't Remember Become The Things You Can't Forget

an object/memoir in verse

Lori Jakiela

ROADSIDE PRESS

Editor: Michele McDannold
Cover Art: Lou Ickes
Author Photo: Phelan Newman

Roadside Press
Meredosia, Illinois

Contents

"The space in which we live should be for the person we are becoming now, not for the person we were in the past."—Marie Kondō, *The Life-Changing Magic of Tidying Up: The Japanese Art of Decluttering and Organizing*

"The creative mind plays with the objects it loves."
—Carl Jung

Prologue: The Object in Question

I had been so focused on what to discard that I had forgotten to cherish the things I loved, the things I wanted to keep.
—Marie Kondo

I find the silver jewelry box—a little tarnished, an etched pair of hearts on top—hidden behind a stash of face masks and hand sanitizers, plastic gloves and Covid tests, all those pandemic leftovers stuffed in a bathroom closet.

I'm purging. *Redding up*, we say in Pittsburgh, which means Spring cleaning, that hope-filled seasonal banishing of dust to dust.

In Sweden, this kind of cleaning is about death—the kind of tidying up people do before dying so as not to burden anyone else with their forgotten to-do lists, unpaid parking tickets, and refrigerator magnets shaped like cat butts.

"Oh dear god, no," a woman I know in New York says about what strangers, or worse, her 83-year-old born-again Christian father, would find in her apartment if something happened on her morning commute.

When people say, "if something happened," they mean dead.

What my New York friend fears: someone finding her pink fuzzy bondage gear and her Picolas Cage vibrator (green, pickle-shaped, with Nic Cage's face on the buzziest part), but mostly her My Little Pony collection.

Adults with My Little Pony collections rank with Disney adults who wear the mouse ears and book their honeymoons at Cinderella's Castle, but don't mind me. I'm judge-y like that.

"I don't know which would be worst," my Little Pony friend says, and makes her own plans to curate the scene of her demise with a proper Swedish Death Cleaning.

In Japan, according to Japanese tidy-master Marie Kondo, such cleaning is less about death or the shame of an adult woman with a vibrating celebrity pickle and several toy ponies named Pinky Pie, and more about shedding earthly concerns.

Such cleaning, according to Marie Kondo, is about sparking joy.

"Keep only those things that speak to your heart," she says.

What my friend fears: giving outsiders insight into what speaks to her heart.

That Pittsburgh phrase, *redding up* has its roots in Middle English. It means "to free." It means "rescue."

"Tidying is the act of confronting yourself," Marie Kondo says, who believes cleanliness will rescue us all.

Marie Kondo, I'd love to peek under your bed.

Marie Kondo, I'd love to reorganize your spice rack.

Marie Kondo, I bet all your socks match.

Marie Kondo, what speaks to your tiny, tidy heart?

I'm sorry, Marie Kondo.

Even your bangs are perfect.

***

For some reason, I've kept this jewelry box, though I can't remember where it came from or who gifted it to me. Maybe it's an age thing. Here in my sixth decade, everything is an age thing.

Until recently, I never thought about how the things I've kept might tell a story about a self I haven't confronted.

Look: here's a worn-out handkerchief and a souvenir penny from Detroit. Here's a tarot deck, a jelly jar filled with safety pins, some funeral cards.

Here's a broken watch, a mood ring, a drawer filled with pink lipsticks with names like Blush, Flamingo, and Ballerina. Here's another drawer filled with more lipstick, one named Vulva, which is for your vagina, and I didn't know that until I got it home.

Look: vibrators—one shaped like a rabbit, one shaped like a bullet.

This feels like a metaphor.

Here's a box of Q-tips, keys from old apartments, a hairbrush tangled with different shades and textures of hair, a note written on a grocery receipt that says, "Eggs."

Here's a jewelry box, dusty, with silver hearts on top.

***

Dear Marie Kondo, purger of purses and pockets, have you no baggage?

Dear Marie Kondo, you white-gloved, spotless, ravaging soul.

For Newman.

Vienna waited until I found you.

On Watching Reruns of Marie Kondo's 2019 Netflix Show
***Tidying Up with Marie Kondo* in 2025**

2019 was a mess, too, remember?
Notre Dame burned and the Amazon
        burned and scientists took a picture
            of a Black Hole that could swallow
                us all.

Today a Harvard scientist says
an alien space probe is on its way.

An MIT scientist says Artificial Intelligence
        will go rogue in a couple years
            and bring on the latest apocalypse

which seems to surprise people despite
those *Terminator* movies when Arnold
        promised he'd be back, and all those *Alien* movies
            that should have taught us something
                useful or at least that in space
                    no one can hear you scream.

I shop for toilet paper on Amazon
        while the Amazon keeps burning
            and millionaire Neil Young
                goes on singing *helpless*
                    helpless into his 80s.

When the earth's closets overflow with stuff
        humans will stash more stuff on Mars.

There are alligators in Pittsburgh's rivers
        not many, but still.

Floods and toppled trees, fires and mudslides.
        "The end times," Aunt Velma says but

Aunt Velma is a Jehovah's Witness.
        She's been tidying up and dreaming
                the end times for years.

"The earth wiped clean," Aunt Velma says
        but she goes on dusting her tiny apartment
                and buying knick-knacks, ceramic poodles
                        with their heads on springs, happy cows
                                with their heads on springs

all of them nodding, nodding
        yes, this is good, yes,
                all is as it should be

keeping her company in this space
        where Aunt Velma plans on spending
                eternity with her fellow believers

which seems crazy, the last
        of humanity holed up

in a Pine Sol-ed senior-citizen high rise
in Trafford, Pennsylvania
but I wish them well.

I don't visit anymore.
I never much liked my aunt
and I like her less now.

My feet hurt.
My knees hurt.
I'm tired and my Starbucks boycott
isn't holding.

I read too much news.
I listen to too much news.
I worry soon there won't be any news.

"Time to lighten up!" Marie Kondo's interpreter
whose name is also Marie says.

The Maries' voices are bubble wrap
and packing peanuts, promising
safe passage to whatever
challenge comes next.

Marie Kondo's method is called KonMari
which sounds like the name of a cruise ship
or a bomber plane or a new cyberweapon.

In the KonMari method, what can't be controlled
        in the world can be controlled
                in a closet. This
                        leads to better
                                mental health, the Maries say.

Time to get out
        the trash bags. Extra large.
                Heavy duty.
                        Biodegradable, if possible.
                                Better to leave
                                        no trace.

I'd forgotten about the jewelry box

those intersected hearts
meant for engraving but left blank.

This makes the box
a perfect re-gift.

Sorry
for all the things

I've re-gifted
in this life.

Sorry
about the candles
and rose-scented soaps.

Sorry
about the tea towels
with sayings like

"Mind Your Biscuits"
and "You've Guac
To Be Kidding Me."

You shouldn't have,
recipients of re-gifts
always say.

Sorry
about the fancy
notebooks, all the pages
blank
where words should be.

You can't put your arms around a memory

That's Johnny Thunders, punk-rock legend
who died, depending, from a drug overdose,
leukemia, or murdered by junkies
who stole his methadone.

Johnny Thunders' neighbor, Willy DeVille,
told reporters Johnny Thunders went out
in "a blaze of glory."

Johnny Thunders' neighbor, Willy DeVille,
told reporters Johnny Thunders had a shit-
ton of methadone, enough to kill for.

Still.

"I thought I might as well make it look real
good, you know, out of respect, so I told
everybody Johnny died on the floor
with his guitar in his hands."

Willy DeVille saw the coroner
take Johnny Thunders' body away.
Rigor mortis had set in, Johnny curled
into a comma, no
guitar in sight.

"I felt bad for everybody,"
Willy DeVille said about why
he said what he said.

"I wanted people
to remember Johnny
as the legend he was."

I can't remember who gifted or re-gifted this jewelry box but I've had it for years

Things you can't remember
become things you can't forget.

Sorry, Johnny Thunders.
That's Tom Waits

whose music I sometimes try
to play by heart

on an out-of-tune piano
I've had since I was a kid.

I have a hard time
playing anything by heart.

I don't trust my memory.
I don't trust my skills.

I have an old
Tom Waits songbook.

It helps some.

The songbook's worn and well-loved
and missing a few pages.

When I say songbook,
I mean my life.

I said that's Tom Waits, but I'm paraphrasing

working
from memory,
so it goes.

So it goes is a phrase
from Kurt Vonnegut's
Slaughterhouse Five.

So it goes is a phrase
that shows up in the book
whenever death is mentioned.

Death is mentioned a lot
in the book, which is about
the bombing of Dresden.

The bombing of Dresden, the most
vicious of World War II bombings,
leveled the city. Nearly everyone died.

Kurt Vonnegut, a prisoner, one
of the greatest witnesses
to the horrors of war, survived

by hiding in a meat locker
in a slaughterhouse
where pigs had been butchered.

So it goes.

Don't quote me
on anything.

Don't trust
anything
now.

Tom Waits

That cigarette wraith,
my personal saint of loss
and nostalgia and longing.

I saw Tom Waits once
in concert, Detroit, Michigan.

His roadies wheeled out a piano
and my heart lifted. Then

they wheeled
the piano back.

"I'm done with all that,"
Tom Waits said.

He did another song
where he clanged
some skillets

then chattered
bicycle chains
across the stage.

There is a beautiful word in Portuguese

Saudade.

Saudade is different from nostalgia
because it can mean longing

for something
that never happened.

Saudade has no direct
English translation.

Saudade encompasses feelings
like melancholy

incompleteness
        wistfulness

                loss
                        love
                                longing.

Longing.

I've said that.

Dada Gaga Ga, Dada Gaga Ga

Maybe Tom Waits' bicycle chains and skillets equal
a deconstructionist dada-ist interpretation
of the beautiful word *saudade*

but

I think the piano
said it better.

"The piano has been drinking,"
Tom Waits sang, "not me."

Sure it has, Tom Waits.
Sure it has.

Memory equals

Recollection. Memory equals
an equation that weighs

someone's or something's
importance in one's life.

I am speaking math now.
I cannot math, and yet

I'm the one
who does my family's taxes.

I'm the one
in charge of our bills.

Forgive me my trespasses, IRS.
Forgive my indiscretions, Quickbooks.

I believe mathing has value
and per this equation I believe

I have value, in that my family
loves and trusts me enough to keep

bill collectors away and the lights on
and all of us moving forward

tightrope walkers
with buttered feet and no net.

Such is my net value/such is my net sum.

Can you speak math,
that surest of languages?

I cannot math thanks to Catholic School
and a nun named Sister Ignatius.

Also, I cannot math
because my brain does not love

numbers or logic or having
to show my work.

Still Sister Ignatius, ruler cocked and ready,
made me do equations

on a chalkboard
in front of the class.

Sister Ignatius, napalm-heart
vicious per her saintly namesake

had another name
for students like me

who could not
math under pressure.

She called us
Cabbage Heads

and hurled chalk-covered erasers
at our vegetating skulls.

Marie Kondo's equation for letting go of the past =

clothes first, plus books, plus
papers, plus miscellany—*komono*—
and lastly, mementos.

Marie Kondo, I, Cabbage Head,
will be buried in a garden
of books, many copies

of *Slaughterhouse Five*
among them. I will be buried
beneath a headstone

of books, with a marker
made of books
that reads:

Fuck off,
Marie Kondo.

Poor Sister Ignatius

I know
it's easy to blame others
for my own moral failures.

Sister Ignatius, you
clearly hated children
as much as Jesus
hated tax collectors.

Tax collectors know a lot
about math but little
about Jesus

and less about children
beyond the Child Credit
Income Tax Break.

Sister Ignatius, if you had your life
to do over, I think
you would have been happier
choosing a different path.

A job with the IRS, maybe
where you could make sure
every Child Credit went to a child

who would, one day, be useful,
who would, one day, math.

Memento Mori

To memorize, from the 1590s on, meant
to commit memory to writing or inscription.

Commit to a person.
Commit a crime.

Commit to memory
or be committed.

Don't you love language?
Don't you love the ebb and flow

of human words
and memory and meaning?

Memento Mori—an object
meant to remind us we will die

something Shakespearean,
a skull, for instance.

Alas, poor Yorick. That most
famous of all Cabbage Heads.

So insignificant he can be
held in the amateur palms

of Shakespearean actors
everywhere.

My high school drama teacher kept a plastic skull on his desk

The skull's name was
The Archbishop of Canterbury

Archie for short.
Archie doubled as a pencil holder.

Archie's jawbone snapped
open and closed.

Archie's jawbone held paper clips
and hall passes and rubber bands.

So it goes, dear Kurt Vonnegut,
who knew death, who knew

the importance of being useful
to the end and beyond, would say.

Henry Chichele, the Real Archbishop of Canterbury

was mostly a sadist who had many people
burned at the stake and yet Henry,
immortalized by Shakespeare, is buried

with great honor and flourish
in a cadaver tomb
in Canterbury Cathedral.

Henry's tomb depicts Henry
both resplendent in life
and as a decaying corpse.

Henry's tomb is meant
to remind visitors of mortality—
memento mori.

Still, only wealthy
and powerful people like Henry
were buried in cadaver tombs.

You can visit the giftshop
and buy refrigerator magnets
and postcards of Henry's tomb

where the inscription reads
"I was pauper-born, then
to primate raised. Now I

am cut down and served up
for worms.
Behold my grave."

"Commit to Memory" Means Learn By Heart

That came years later though,
in the Year of Our Lord 1838.

1838.
What a promising year, those double eights.

Eight, the symbol of eternity.
An eight toppled on its side goes on and on.

Eight—lucky in numerology.
Eight—a new beginning, material wealth, power.

Eight—a racetrack to eternity,
an endless knot.

The Buddhists and their Eight Auspicious Symbols,
two linked golden fishes, a conch shell, a treasure vase.

The last time the number 1838 hit the lottery
was April 21, 2025.

The lottery was the Dhana Nidhanaya
from Sri Lanka.

There were
no winners.

Consider the perfection of a figure eight

Consider an ice skater in the 1980s
committed to mastering that feat

on an Olympic-sized ice rink
in the middle of a suburban mall

let's say Monroeville Mall
in Monroeville, Pennsylvania.

Consider the ice skater, alone
in the center of the rink,

spinning like a ballerina
in a music box.

Consider the children and couples
toddling the rink's edge. Consider

the coaches and shoppers who judge
each spin between sips of Orange Julius.

Consider Orange Julius, that mystery drink.
Part orange juice, part milk, part sugar, part magic.

Not a smoothie, not a milkshake, not a blended
juice but something unnatural and all its own.

Such was the landscape of my youth.

Imagine an ice palace where a food court now stands

Imagine a failed food court filled
with Vacancy signs and pop-up stores

with names like BOUGIE JUICE and 14K!!
Imagine temporary casinos with machines

that look legit but never hit.
Imagine senior citizens like me

in sensible sneakers
and compression socks

doing our zombie laps
heads down and dreaming

our past loves and lives,
Fitbits clocking our every step.

Things Remembered

When I was 17, I worked at Things
Remembered in Monroeville Mall.

Things Remembered—a specialty store
where you could buy a *memento mori*—

a skull ring or a wallet chain
with an engravable coffin charm, or

a silver jewelry box lined in red velvet
with blank hearts on top.

Things Remembered—on the top floor
of Monroeville Mall, overlooking the ice rink.

"They'll never forget you," the Things Remembered
slogan said, "when you shop at Things Remembered."

Engraving Things at Things Remembered

was a serious handheld operation
but everything I engraved
would have been impossible to re-gift.

Everything I engraved looked scribbled
by zombies, who,
zombies being zombie, dropped
fingers like bird seed
and couldn't spell
for shit.

Dawn of the Dead

Monroeville Mall, Monroeville, Pennsylvania
home to an Olympic ice palace and
the setting for the movie *Dawn of the Dead.*

Monroeville Mall, Monroeville, Pennsylvania
is zombie-famous.

You might remember the posters:

"When there's no more room
      in HELL
         the dead will walk
            the EARTH."

Or at least they'll walk Monroeville Mall
every year for the memorial Zombie Walk

when fans travel the world over
to shred their clothes and cover themselves

in fake blood and peeling skin
and stumble around, muttering

"Brains.
      I need brains."

Bunch of cabbage heads,
Sister Ignatius would say.

The zombies in *Dawn of the Dead*
are, like the senior citizen mall walkers,

more or less,
starving.

Rotten Tomatoes

If you haven't seen *Dawn of the Dead*—that brainy
critique of late-stage capitalism and consumerism
with its Santa zombies and biker zombies and zombies
disguised as mannequins who lash out at brain-deficient
consumers idling over purchases at shops like
Things Remembered—

it's awesome.
Five stars.
Totally recommend.

Glitter Glue

I was so bad at engraving names
on I.D. bracelets at Monroeville Mall
when engraving names on I.D. bracelets
was the peak expression of eternal love
I was reassigned
to glitter glue.

I wrote people's names
in glue on Christmas stockings.
Then I smothered
the goo-names in glitter.

I'd write "Bob"
and it would come out "Blob."
I'd write "Ashley"
and it would come out "Assly".

My gig at Things Remembered
was a seasonal one.

I wasn't invited back.

The woman who works the 14K!! looks expensive
in her shiny gold jumpsuit. Her eyelashes

could double as porch awnings. Her lips
look stung by wasps.

She pokes a fake fingernail loaded
with sticky gold goo on my cheek.

It burns.

"This will perk you
right up," she says, and smiles

but her face
doesn't move much.

The gold goo on the woman's finger
is meant to erase years.

The gold goo on the woman's finger
is meant to fill in wrinkles, sadness, loss.

Watch out for this woman.

She'll make you feel bad
about everything.

P.S.

Later, the spot where the woman
stuck my face with sticky gold goo
breaks out in a rash.

Regrets. I've Had a Few

"I wouldn't change a thing
about my life except my bank balance,"

Johnny Thunders said
days before he died.

My friend Joe used to get drunk and argue

with inanimate objects. He'd point at an ashtray on the bar
—remember ashtrays?—and say,

"This fucking ashtray will outlive you.
It will outlive me.

This fucking piece of plastic will go on and on
when we're dead and buried. Fuck you, ashtray!"

And then he'd order another beer and check his reflection
in the mirror over the bar. Then

he'd order another beer.
And another.

I get it.
Not judging.

My stashed jewelry box doubles as a music box

Someone chose this velvet-lined box, its song
to gift to me, maybe.

Also, the box has enough silver in it
to tarnish, which would have made it

top shelf
at Things Remembered.

What kind of person forgets
the origins of such a thing

that's clearly designed
to last?

"Cabbage Head,"
Sister Ignatius would say

and let her erasers
fly.

**I read somewhere you can use ketchup
to leech tarnish off silver**

though I haven't tried that yet. Leeching
tarnish off silver makes it sparkle.

"You'll look ten years younger!"
the 14K!! woman with the goo-finger said,

then she slathered me up, an object, a mark,
a thing she needed to get her commission

or however they pay people
for making other people

confront mortality in the middle
of a dying suburban mall.

As for the jewelry box, the ketchup approach
seems sticky and messy when there are

all sorts of tidier cancer-causing chemical
alternatives that would work better, I bet

if one cared about such things.
Which I do not.

Which I
do not.

The best things come to those who wait

That's a Heinz ketchup slogan.

Heinz is the official ketchup of Pittsburgh
my home country, though the company abandoned
the city for Ohio years ago.

For a while Heinz Ketchup's theme song was "Anticipation"
by Carly Simon, whose chorus reminded listeners
that these are the good old days, moments to savor,
ketchup and memories being delicious and timeless.

To get Heinz ketchup out of a glass bottle faster,
because who has time to anticipate ketchup,
the trick was to whack the spot on the bottle
etched with the number 57—

57 for Heinz's 57 Varieties, though
the actual number of Heinz products
at the company's 1896 founding was 60.

5 was H.J. Heinz's lucky number.
7 was his wife's lucky number.

Marketing.
The power of numbers.

Mathing, dear Sister Ignatius,
you terrible human, rest in peace.

Heinz's first product wasn't ketchup

It was grated horseradish.
Hardly anyone likes horseradish these days.

These days Heinz ketchup bottles are mostly plastic.
You can squeeze the ketchup out.

No anticipation.
No challenge.

Who has time to wait
for anything now?

On finding out that the music box I found stashed in my closet plays the theme from *Cats*

I don't remember winding it up before
though I'm sure I must have.

I don't know why I'd forget such a thing,
Cats being both terrible and unforgettable.

The musical ran for 21 years
on London's West End, 18 years on Broadway.

Cats clawed its way into 19 languages,
spawned 89 global performances

and starred Dame Judy Dench
and Taylor Swift, who both brought sexy back

in their catsuits but in vastly different
and cross-generational ways.

Dame Dench, you eternal hottie. Taylor,
you sweetheart, you have years to go.

Cats with its Jellicles and Heavisides
and hand-painted catsuits is more or less

as off-putting as horseradish but audiences
keep coming anyway.

T.S. Eliot, the author of "The Wasteland",
would be appalled maybe over the success

of this, his jokester work, or
maybe not a joke

maybe a rip-off of something
T.S. Eliot wrote on acid if T.S. Eliot

did acid (see "The Wasteland," which may
make a pro-acid argument for T.S. Eliot's genius).

I kind of hate T.S. Eliot.

Cats was the first real musical
I ever saw.

It took me too long to get
the irony of that.

Sorry for what I said about horseradish

It's delicious and may help prevent
cancer and heart disease and Alzheimer's.

Ancient Greeks said horseradish
like 14K!! goo is worth its weight
in gold.

What Was Your First Real Anything?

Admitting *Cats* is my first real theater experience
is up there with naming my first concert.

People ask that question all the time.
"What was your first *real* concert?"

The people who ask that question
have a collection of concert t-shirts and ticket stubs

and cool first-concert answers they're waiting
to pull out like winning lottery numbers.

"The Stones," they say. "Bruce," they say.
"*The River*. Not *Born in the U.S.A.*"

One 70-year-old hipster I know
says her first concert was The Doors.

She says Jim Morrison peed off the edge
of the stage and that his pee

arced in a perfect stream
right into her pink and eager mouth.

She wrote a poem about it, which is
supposed to be testimony

that her story is true, that her memory
is pure reportage, poetry being truer than truth.

She's 72 and wears designer biker jackets
and enough jewelry to draw a lightning strike.

I believe Jim Morrison peed from the stage.
He did that a lot, I think.

What I doubt is that Jim Morrison—drunk,
stoned—ever had that kind of aim.

Poets, man.

One True Thing

My first concert was Shaun Cassidy,
"Da Doo Ron Ron."

My father took me.

Cats, Toronto, Canada, Circa 1980s

I was in my 20s, about to make many mistakes
I'd spend decades trying to un-make.

Remember your 20s?
I hope yours were better than mine.

Remember 25—the mathing, the panic,
a quarter century old!

Beware 25.
Beware the mathing of your life.

Cats, Toronto, Canada, Circa 1980s, 2

I saw *Cats* on a trip with a man I'd marry
then divorce within months.

Aside from choosing *Cats*
none of this was his fault.

The man I'd marry was kind and handsome

a good amateur rugby player
who grilled great steaks.

Grilling great steaks seemed
a marriageable skill

even though when I met him
I was a vegetarian.

I believed in time then. I believed
there was a time to settle.

How he felt, I didn't know, not really.
I like to think he believed

grilling a steak was a prerequisite
for a good marriage.

I like to think he believed
in settling too.

Most people settle

the way the earth settles, a house settles,
debts settle. Settling means
peace, acceptance.
Settling in math-speak equals
a grown-up thing. Resolute.
To resolve or make an agreement.
To become comfortable.
To make calm or quiet.
To settle one's affairs.
To settle into the earth like a corpse. *Behold!*
To gradually sink under one's own weight.

Cabbage Heads, Sister Ignatius
herself a settler, maybe, said
and hurled her erasers
at our stupid
settling skulls.

Maybe Sister Ignatius was a saint and not a monster

Maybe she was trying to save all of us
Cabbage Heads from our mistakes

by throwing those erasers
laden with chalk dust, a visible blessing

like priests do on Ash Wednesday
when they press their thumbs

into ashes and smudge them
on the foreheads of the faithful.

*Remember you are dust
and to dust you shall return.*

Remember, Sister Ignatius might
have said, *you are mistakes*

and to mistakes you shall return.
Again and again.

Erase. Erasure. The beautiful
promise and possibility of that.

Bless you on the back end
of this life, Sister Ignatius.

I'm sorry I made fun
of your mustache.

**Love, impermanent as glue-glitter, Love, an
unsolvable equation**

I'd already been in love, the heart-and-atom-smashing
tender-shoot kind, and stayed in bed for months

settling under my own thinning weight, such is the luxury
of being young and heartbroken with parents

who'd keep paying my rent and a college that didn't pull
my scholarship no matter how few classes I attended.

At 25, carrying my new world-weariness to a job
in public relations where I was paid to smile

I knew I never wanted
to feel that way again.

And so, when the man I'd marry organized
a party with his family and rugby mates

when he got down on one knee
with his mother's ring in front of a bonfire

his rugby pals built while butting heads and chanting
magical rugby things, when he asked me to marry him,

knowing as he did how much I hated to spoil a party,
I said, *sure, why not.*

I rehearsed
those words, Carly Simon sang.

The only things I know are treble, volume,
and reverb, Johnny Thunders said.

Helpless, helpless, Neil Young sang
when he left his wife for Darryl Hannah

who once played a mermaid
in a ridiculous rom-com.

Cabbage Heads, Sister Ignatius said,
and threw up her helpless, empty hands.

In Toronto, before *Cats*—we had reservations

at a fancy restaurant overlooking the city. I pocketed
a pack of fancy cigarettes in a gold-edged box.

Canada had wonderful cigarettes and everyone
smoked in a way that seemed French

though I had never been to France
and did not know anyone French.

I didn't actually smoke
and back then Canada

didn't require a passport
but seemed far away as Mars.

"Nothing lasts," I said more than once
to my new fiancée,

that strange French word
that never seemed to fit.

The cigarettes were lovely though.
I pretended to inhale. I tilted my head

and blew smoke and imagined I looked
grown and sexy while I tried not to choke.

At the restaurant, I ordered lobster, my first

I didn't think about the bill.
I wasn't paying.
I didn't pay for the cigarettes I fake smoked
or for the *Cats* tickets, or for the nice hotel room
and room service
and while I considered myself
a feminist, I was ready to give over
to my age-appropriate life
as a married grown woman
who might never see Paris
and who had never been
a mermaid but who had these
French-seeming cigarettes
and who was prepared
for the disappointment
she knew was at the heart
of every experience
she wouldn't have to pay for.

"Buy the ticket, take the ride."

That's Hunter S. Thompson.
But Hunter got stomped
by the Hell's Angels
when he was so cheap
he refused to share

the stash of beer he kept hidden
in the trunk of his car.

I love Hunter S. Thompson
because he wrote like a devil
infected with god.

But Hunter S. Thompson
was, in short,
an asshole.

I was
in short
an asshole.

Waiting

The waiter at the fancy Toronto restaurant
took our order. He poured lemon water in goblets.

He brought champagne.
He presented hot towels

and had to demonstrate how to use
the towels to freshen our hands.

And then he did a meet-and-greet
with me and my lobster.

He brought this sad creature to the table
where I sat making small talk with this man

I agreed to spend the rest of my life
making small talk with.

The waiter said,
"Is this satisfactory, madam?"

I was 25 years old.
A quarter century.

Madam?

It sounded wrong, too old, but also

I wanted it, that grown feeling.

I wanted to believe
in my own judgment, my own

ability to make decisions that were,
in short, fucked.

I wanted to conjure
the willpower to live with that.

I must have nodded and smiled.
"Is this satisfactory, madam?"

Yes, this is satisfactory.
Yes, this is fine.

Some facts about lobsters

Lobsters, scientists say, are highly intelligent creatures.
Lobsters, scientists say, can live up to 100 years or more.

Lobsters, scientists say, feel pain and can't go into shock
which means lobsters boiled alive suffer

the most inhumane
death imaginable.

Lobsters, scientists say, feel love
and walk claw in claw with their beloved forever.

Scientists who understand lobsters
say no one should eat lobsters

ever, no matter how delicious, no matter
the longing, no matter how hungry.

**When the lobster, my lobster, my first lobster, looked
at me**

it wriggled its antennae back and forth, a message,
a kind of crustacean Morse Code that translated
to *help*,
          to *seriously*, to *no*,
               to *you're fucking kidding me*,
                   to *oh come on*,
                       to *you heartless fucking*
            bitch.

        You heartless.
            Fucking.
                Sad.
                     Human.

Bitch.

What I don't remember as well—

the man I would marry, what he said, what
he did, how he looked in that moment.

But the lobster.
The waiter.

The waiter had a French accent,
Quebecois probably. He seemed

European because Toronto and because
of those cigarettes ubiquitous enough

every Canadian cab driver
offered me one.

The waiter, who presented the lobster to me,
an offering, a burning bridge to cross.

*If you do this there will be
no undoing it.* The waiter, clean

white starched cloth over his arm
white starched apron

over his black suit, a priest
presiding over a covenant.

The lobster flailing, a sacrifice
on its lovely silver tray.

"Is this satisfactory, madam?"
Is this what you wanted even so?

Yes, this is satisfactory.
Yes, this is fine.

Every once in a while a lobster in a fancy restaurant escapes

or is rescued—redded up
by a well-meaning patron
who takes the lobster home
and puts it in a tank fit for a lobster.

The lobster, alone, lonely
doesn't adapt well.

A lobster is not a pet. A lobster longs
for connection, another compatible
lobster to live out its forever days
or to lock claws with at least.

Ode to His Holiness, James St. James

The waiter in his black suit and white bow tie
reminded me of my college roommate's
black-and-white cat James St. James

who loved to bring offerings—dead mice mostly—and leave them
on the pillow next to me in my first heartbreak break-up bed
when I didn't have the energy or desire to rise.

"Oh, he loves you!" my roommate said
about the corpses that lay next to me
like severed horse heads.

My roommate was sweet
and encouraging and worried
over me, despite me.

I don't remember getting up
to remove the dead mice
her cat brought.

I don't remember raising myself
like a zombie to walk the earth
and bury the bodies of these

tiny creatures or drop them in the trash.
My roommate must have done that, too.
Bless her. Bless her.

And bless you
James St. James,
you saintly feral feline.

Apologia

I'm sorry.
I'm sorry and sorry
and sorry.

I am sorry for the hurt I caused.
And yet it's not simple regret I'm writing about.
There may be no word for the feelings I have.

Saudade, maybe.
Loss. Longing. Nostalgia.
Even for the pain of first heartbreak.

I remember feeling so deeply
that nothing—not a phone ringing,
not a bill collector, not hunger

or thirst or a tiny dead thing
bleeding on my pillow
could make me rise.

I remember the freedom to feel
so intensely without pause, without
regret, without explanation.

Saudade.
The longing for the pain of youth.
The longing for loss, that, even so.

"Lovely," I said

to the waiter.
I hope the word caught
like smoke in my throat.

I hope I hesitated
even a little.

*We had the experience
but missed
the meaning.*

That's Jemima, the youngest, most innocent
least annoying kitten in *Cats* singing
"Moments of Happiness."

Cats is terrible, but
there are a few
salvageable things.

My memory of the man I would marry

Of course
he was present.

Of course
he paid the bill.

Of course
he planned this trip and held my hand

through Grizabella, the one-time glamour cat's version
of "Memory," then Jemima's follow-up version

of "Memory" and then through the curtain rising version
of "Memory."

Why I have so little memory
of his face, or his voice unsettles me.

I like to think if I passed him on the street
I'd recognize him now, yes, of course but

I'm not certain. What I remember:
the waiter, the lobster.

The way it looked at me. So
vulnerable. The way it came back

under a silver dome the waiter lifted
and presented with a flourish.

Voila.
There it is.

There you are.
Look. See.

Isn't this
what you wanted?

Delicacy

The waiter cracked the shell with a flourish,
and pulled out the sweet tender meat
and showed me the best parts.

"The green is a delicacy," he said,
"Tomalley."

The waiter's hands were soft, pale,
long-fingered underwater things.

I remember my first love
but not the man I left him for.

I remember the waiter's hands
but not the hands of the man
I would marry.

I remember the feel
of the fine linen napkin
dabbing at my lips

and a forkful of lobster,
dripping with butter.

I have no memory of my fiancé's mouth.
I have no memory of my tongue in his mouth

his mouth on my breasts, his tongue inside me
my name in his mouth, his name in my mouth

the vows we said and repeated, all of it
disembodied, dismembered, disremembered.

I'm thinking of him as I write this
but I rarely think of him, not even

when I have lobster, which I love,
a cruel and terrible choice,

delicious
even so.

An Aside

Tomalley,
mostly a lobster's liver and pancreas
can be poisonous.

Paralytic shellfish poisoning
causes numbness, confusion.
All the things time does, too.

Because the Internet

I looked him up on Facebook
and Instagram a few times.

His profile picture
is a motorcycle.

I never knew him
to ride one.

Marie Kondo Has a Question

Can you truthfully say
you treasure something
buried so deeply
in a cupboard or drawer
that you have forgotten
its existence?

Decades later

I'm married again.
I tell people it's my first time.

A lie, I know.
Unfair, I know.

I have been married for over 25 years
and counting to a man I love
so much it hurts to admit how much.

How vulnerable that is.
How terrifying.

*I never want to feel that way
ever again.* I hear my young self,
taken to her bed, say and yet

here I am.

Tomalley—
the tender underbelly.

Tomalley—
the not-lovely dangerous
exquisite sweetness.

Memories

Inside the jewelry box that is also a music box
I've stashed memories—snippets

of my children's hair from their first haircuts,
the hospital band clipped from my newborn daughter's wrist,

the hospital band clipped from my newborn son's wrist,
both tiny enough to fit on my ring finger.

And there are teeth. Lots of teeth.
My son and daughter's baby teeth.

A little dried blood
at the roots.

There are dead insects in there, too.
Larvae and silverfish, I think, so gross

and drawn to decay, I know, but
I don't disturb them.

They look like tiny lobsters.

This Little Light of Mine

My friend K kept her daughter's teeth in a baggie.
Later, K took the teeth to a candle-making class.

She poured wax over the teeth and made a candle,
a gift for her daughter, who hasn't burned it.

The candle's scent is Birthday Cake.
The wax is dotted with teeth and sprinkles.

"Creepy," K's daughter said about the gift
which she keeps in a box in her closet.

Tiny Teeth

When my young son had a loose tooth
he freaked out. He worried about pain.
He worried about everything.
We started to call blood "tooth juice."
My husband came up with that name.
My son believed, and it made things
easier for a while, for a few teeth, amen.

Our son, never a sucker
for the tooth fairy, needed first
a dollar a tooth, then two dollars
then up. Such is the math
of capitalism and wisdom
and parenthood and pain.

By the time our daughter, four
years younger, started losing
her baby teeth, she had the deal
figured out.
She wanted
the whole ceremony—
the tooth fairy notes and drawings
my husband made that became
the Tooth Fairy's signature for years.

Instead of freaking out, my daughter,
discovering a loose tooth, would reach

into her mouth and pull.
"Bada-Boom," she'd say
and hold up the tooth like a prize.

We started calling her mouth a bank.
The price for a tooth was up
to $5 and soon she was raking it in.

When I count the teeth
in the jewelry box, I do the math—
40 teeth, 20 each, at an average of
say $3 a tooth equals $120 dollars
equals priceless.

"Good job, Cabbage Head,"
Sister Ignatius would say,
then double-check my work.

Snippets

My son's first haircut was in Michigan and we took my husband's parents and grandfather as witnesses. The salon specialized in kids cuts. "No tears, no fears," the sign out front said.

My son sat on a smiling T-Rex as the hairdresser wrapped a plastic cape around his shoulders. She said, "There. You're a superhero."

"I know," my son said, but he flinched when the hairdresser snipped a tiny lock of blonde hair out of his eyes, then handed the snippet to me, which at some point I stashed into the heart box.

I don't remember my daughter's first haircut, but I remember her curls—so blonde they glowed.

"What a beautiful child," strangers would say.

They'd stop me in grocery stores, first with my son then with my daughter, and for a minute we'd all hold still, bathed in the love of strangers, in the store's immortal flickering fluorescent lights.

Allen Ginsberg

"The mind remembers
that which is vivid. The mind
remembers that which is good."

That's Allen Ginsberg, who never
had children and lied
about many things

but offered permission
for artists and writers to believe
our memories hold value.

Allen Ginsberg once signed
his *Collected Poems* for me.
Allen Ginsberg's *Collected Poems*

is thick as a phone book
though most people remember
only "Howl" and "Kaddish."

Along with his signature
Allen Ginsberg drew a dragon
with huge hairy balls, such

is the unforgettable legacy
of dear Allen Ginsberg.

**The jewelry box, the object of this memoir, this found
forgotten thing**

was it a gift from the man I married years ago?
Maybe.
I don't think so.
Maybe.
That I can't remember will be something
I'll have to puzzle through.

More likely the music box was something
I brought home and gave to my mother
who loved *Cats* and would appreciate a gift
her daughter brought home
with an employees' discount
from Things Remembered and didn't want
to disfigure it
by trying to engrave it herself.

More likely it was something I saved
when my mother died, when I was grieving
and lost, and somehow her space became a space
for me to hold everything I didn't want to lose.

You can't put your arms around a memory,
Johnny Thunders sang, but here
is something to hold.

Don't try, said Johnny Thunders,
who died, people said, with his guitar
held tight in his arms.

The Things You Can't Remember Become The Things You Can't Forget

My husband and I have two children.
My parents are dead, but I have two in-laws.

Such a strange phrase, in-laws.
So close to outlaws. How funny is that?

My father-in-law, Charlie, has dementia.
He's forgotten many things but remembers others.

What he's forgotten—his favorite order at restaurants.
The names of salad dressings. The names

of his neighbors. How long
he's been married. How to work a zipper.

What he remembers—Frank Sinatra, Sinatra's world
every time we're together.

"It's a beautiful day," Charlie says, then sings.
 "Why don't we do this more often?"

What he remembers—how a good meal feels
in his body. Ice cream. Coney Island. Growing up

in the Bronx, a three-story walk-up.
His father's vegetable garden.

What he remembers—25-cent movies, Superman,
popcorn with real butter. The rattle of the subway.

The lights of New York after dark. His nickname, Lemon.
His years of working, feeling useful, feeling loved.

"The mind remembers that which is vivid. The mind remembers
that which is good," Allen Ginsberg, that beatnik genius, said.

"Life is," Charlie said to me the other day, pausing
to search for the word, "life."

It's something he heard from the birds that speak to him now.
The birds have traveled everywhere. They know things.

Charlie believes birds are angels, messengers.
Keepers of memory.

Maybe they are.
I believe they are.

Publication Notes

In *Misfit Magazine,* Alan Catlin, editor: "On Watching Re-
runs of Marie Kondo's 2019 Netflix Show 'Tidying Up with
Marie Kondo' in 2025," "The Things You Can't Remember
Become the Things You Can't Forget," and "My Friend Joe
Used to Get Drunk and Argue."

Lori Jakiela is the author of eight books, most recently *ALL SKATE: True Stories from Middle Life* (Roadside Press, 2025). Her work has been widely published in *The New York Times*, *The Washington Post*, *Brevity*, *Pittsburgh Magazine*, *Pittsburgh Quarterly*, *The Chicago Tribune* and more. Her awards include The Saroyan Prize for International Literature from Stanford University, The City of Asylum-Pittsburgh Prize, The Wicked Woman Prize from Brickhouse Books, and more. She lives in Trafford, Pennsylvania, and teaches writing at The University of Pittsburgh-Greensburg and The Pittsburgh Theological Seminary. Her author website is http://lorijakiela.net.

MORE ROADSIDE PRESS TITLES

The Broken Buddha * Johnny Cordova

Things to Say When You Have Nothing to Say * Kerry Trautman

Everything I Touch Is—& Isn't—You * David Allen Sullivan &

Ignatius Valentine Aloysius

Dope and Vodka and Cigarettes, and Not Shaving Her Legs * Dave Newman

Some Kind of Instinct

When Fran in *Dawn of the Dead*
asks Stephen in *Dawn of the Dead* why
zombies keep flocking
to Monroeville Mall
Stephen
pauses.

"Some
kind of instinct," he says.
"Memory
of what
        they used to do."

Things Remembered carried jewelry boxes

like the one I've kept stashed, but still
I don't remember where I got mine.

It must have been a gift, but
I have no memory of the gifting.

That I've kept it without wondering
seems strange.

That I've kept it without wondering
has me thinking.

I'm 60. I worry about forgetting things
like my car keys or license plate or my life.

"You look tired," the woman at the 14K!! stand
in the Monroeville Mall Food Court says.

The 14K!! stand specializes in anti-aging
skin care made with real 14-carat gold flakes.

"It's expensive," the poster on the 14K!! stand says
"because you're worth your weight in gold."

I weigh a lot more
than I used to.